Encouraging Words for Discouraging Times

James & Yvonne Bailey

Encouraging Words for Discouraging Times

Copyright © 2016 by Yvonne Bailey

Created4hp123@yahoo.com

Cover Design: Cover Creator, Create Space
Editorial: Jeff Hill, Quilldrivers
Image drawn by: Thomas Jones

ISBN-10:0-692-61789-2
ISBN-13:978-0-692-61789-2

Available on Kindle and other devices.

Dedication

This book is dedicated to our family and friends who continue to believe even when life says something differently. For we walk by faith daily and our daily faith works by love.

Thanks Dad! It's Done! Multiply!

Table of Contents

Introduction

Therefore humble yourselves under the mighty hand of God, that He may exalt you in due time, casting all your care upon Him, for He cares for you. 1 Peter 5:6,7 (NKJV)

Introduction

When a person is set free from the lifestyle that accompanies a heroin addiction, the change is no small thing. Pastor James L. Bailey experienced such a drastic deliverance from heroin's power. Motivated by God's love and the drastic change, he began a journey to share God's love with anyone he came in contact with. He shared as a prophet, evangelist, pastor, and teacher. He shared as a son, husband, father, brother, uncle, grandfather, and friend. He shared whenever and wherever there was an opportunity.

The following pages contain letters of encouragement that were sent to inmates in prisons and jails all over the United States. Pastor James wanted others to embrace God's love greater than he had, and he wanted to see captive hearts set free with the Good News of Jesus Christ. It did not matter where the person was, all that mattered was the willingness to let Jesus come in and do what He does best in a surrendered heart.

Individually, we may not be physically incarcerated in a correctional facility; but we can be spiritually, emotionally, and mentally bound to a lifestyle of habits and thinking that keep us going around the same old mountain, day after day, month after month, and year after year. We want to do something different, but we don't know how. It takes courage to admit I need a change. It takes courage to admit I am not who I want to be. It takes much courage to want to make a change and trust God to help you become all He has created you to be.

Please allow the written words and the Holy Spirit to speak to you as you read. Be open to do what He tells you to do. He loves you very much. No habit of any kind is more powerful than the power of His forgiving and transforming love.

Encouraging Words for Discouraging Times can be the key that unlocks your prison doors. Take courage and use the key. I took courage and I'm glad I did.

Yvonne Bailey

Section One

Encouraging words for eternal change

JUNKIE TO JESUS

Dear Reader,

God has done great things for me and is very compassionate toward me. In my childhood I was raised in a somewhat normal home. My mother saw to it that we attended church every Sunday. Although I heard about Jesus Christ, I only remember one time when I asked Him to forgive me: I had gotten caught stealing cherries from a cherry tree. In our after-school Bible class, a little old lady asked was there anyone who would like Jesus to forgive them and I said yes.

As I progressed in life, I believe I went through the normal changes from adolescent to teen years. Yet during these years I had a lot of unanswered questions in my life. Who was I? Where was I headed? What was my purpose?

When I was a teenager, a riot broke out in Detroit. Following the riot, came a flood of drugs. Kids in junior high and high school began to experiment with drugs. I resisted the temptation and held off from participating for a while. But because of insecurities, peer pressure, and unanswered questions, I yielded. There was a voice that called out and said, "Stand up, James." Not knowing where the voice came from caused confusion. I didn't want to stand with the guys on the streets, I couldn't relate to them. I couldn't stand up with those in the church because I didn't really know Jesus. I couldn't stand with those in school because of low esteem. And I didn't believe my family understood me. I was confused!

While attending a church function, I saw a deacon drinking at the bar and said, "If he can drink, I can drink too." So, I started to drink beer. One day the fellows asked me to go out with them to get high. I remember saying, "I don't care! I don't care," then I went out and got high. I know now that I was fighting against the voice of the Holy Spirit, warning me not to go in that direction. Later on that evening a voice came to me and this time I looked up and said, "I accept you." Little did I realize that this voice was not from God, and it was like I entered the twilight zone. A whole world was opened to me and I began to understand the language of the streets. I walked and talked like the guys on the street. (I later learned that I had become possessed with a demon spirit.)

I went from iniquity to iniquity, progressively getting worse and worse. The wicked things I did began to scare me. I found myself hopelessly lost and strung out on drugs. It was as if I was on a fast merry-go-round and couldn't get off. Something had control over my life. I was bound and strung out. My car was repossessed and we had received an eviction notice because I was using the rent money for drugs. I left my pregnant wife, and my life had hit rock bottom. The FBI was after me and told me I was going to jail for federal check fraud offenses. The pressure was tremendous. My life was a wreck. The devil told me, If you kill yourself, you'll escape all this. I believed him and attempted many times to kill myself. I even thought about shooting rat poison in my veins. After many failed attempts, I found myself hungry, all alone, and wandering the streets.

I walked into a small church to keep warm. The preacher made an announcement that there was a clinic available for anyone who needed a place to stay, food to eat, and a habit to kick. That was ME! Through this divine intervention of God, He sent church people to minister to me in this clinic. For the first time in my life, I heard the gospel of Jesus Christ, how He died for my sins. That if I would surrender my life to Him, He would give me a new life.

While in the clinic, there was an event that really blew my mind. The same little old lady from my childhood came in telling the same story about Jesus Christ and that I needed to be saved. I knew this was not a coincidence. So, during one of the services, the call was made and the woman spoke of Nicodemus and how he secretly went to Jesus by night and Jesus declared to him, "You must be born again." She also said that if I don't turn to God, I would be filled with my own ways. (Proverbs 1:31) I did not want to be filled with my own ways.

I came trembling before God and saw and felt a light shining brighter than the sun. God was trying to get in touch with me, but I closed my eyes and turned away. With my head bowed to the floor I said, "I'm not ready. I don't want to become a religious fanatic." The devil told me, "That's not God, that's only the light fixture." I said, "Yeah, that's not God." Yet as I

9

looked towards the floor, the light was shining bright from the ground up. I said, "This can't be the light fixture. God wants to change my life." My heart was smitten and I said, "God, I surrender all." When I said that, the light entered me (Jesus is the Light of the world). I began to shake and something sinister left out of me. The lady told me later, as she prayed for me, a force went past her so strong, and she had to double back. When Jesus came in, the devil had to leave! I could see as if it was red blood that started from the top of my head like a giant eraser covering me and it took away all my sins. I was washed clean! I was changed in the twinkle of an eye! One moment I was insane, drug-infested, and burdened down. The next instant I was clean, pure, as if I never sinned in my life. The heavy weight of guilt was lifted off me and I knew instantly I did not have to do drugs any longer.

The desire to steal, lie, and curse was gone. That racing mind left me. I received a new desire to read the Bible, to pray and learn about Jesus Christ. My craving for the world left. The Bible declares if any man be in Christ, he is a new creature. Old things have passed away, behold all things become new. (2 Corinthians 5:17)

Since the time of receiving Jesus Christ as my personal Savior, my life has not been the same. God restored my marriage. I got full-time employment. Much of the respect I lost was reestablished because of God's grace on my life. The same people that repossessed my car financed another one. I faced many of the problems I was running from, but this time Jesus was with me. The charges the FBI had against me were eventually dropped as Jesus showed Himself to me as a great lawyer. Jesus changed my life from despair to joy. He turned darkness and hopelessness to light with a bright eternal outlook on life. He has not finished working with and in me and I see and know there are greater things ahead of me.

Note:

From Junkie to Jesus were the words that riveted from the heart of Pastor James. His life exhibited what the transforming power of God can do in a heart that is totally surrendered to Jesus. He not only surrendered himself, but he commanded his household to seek after God and serve the Lord. His wife and five children also received Christ and worked together reaching the lost for Christ. But even in the middle of temptations and struggles of life, he was always declaring that once he was addicted to heroin, but Jesus set him free for all eternity.

This message of hope was the platform on which he stood to encourage those, in or outside, of correctional facilities, that there is an eternal hope waiting just for you! Receive Jesus as the Savior and Master of your life and you will never be the same.

The encouraging words that follow are just a few of the many messages he shared with whoever was willing to listen. He was not ashamed of the Gospel of Jesus Christ for it is the power of God unto salvation to everyone who believes. (Romans 1:16)

As you read, expect the Spirit of God to begin to talk and commune with you. Don't argue or try to figure anything out, just surrender and embrace the encouraging words of truth.

The salvation of Pastor James L. Bailey took place February 9, 1973 and he continued to serve Christ until his home going on April 15, 2008.

Section Two

Encouraging words for assurance

LOCATE YOURSELF!

Here are a few questions that can help you to determine if you know Christ or think you know Him:

1. When did you meet Jesus? (Become born again)

2. Have you been baptized in water since you believed? (Buried with Christ)

3. Have you been baptized in the Holy Ghost? (Filled with the Spirit)

4. Are you a member of a Bible believing church? (Part of a local body)

5. Do you tithe? (Give to God)

6. How often do you pray? (Talk to God and He talks to you)

7. Do you consistently read your Bible? (Life's instruction manual)

8. Do you tell others about Christ? (Magnify God and His goodness to you)

9. Do you serve others? (In your home, church, job, or community)

10. What can you do to make changes in your life? (Depend upon the Word and wisdom of God)

Many are looking for the supernatural zapping of the Holy Spirit to get rid of the desires that cause us to draw away from God. But when the temptation comes and the desires come, there is no defense. You had an experience with Christ, but no foundation was made in living the Word of God daily. There must be a connection with the living Word of God and the way you live. The truth and revelation of God's Word will definitely set you free.

You shall know the truth and the truth shall set you free. (John 8:32)

Being born again is the start of a brand new life. You begin to live a life that you have never lived before, you walk in paths you have not walked before, and see things in a way you have never seen before.

There is nothing ordinary with an encounter with the King of the Universe. Your life will never be the same and the fruit of the Spirit will begin to operate in your life. Many of you can testify how you felt when Christ became the center of your life. There was a newness and a freshness that you had only dreamed about, but for the first time in your life, you knew that God was real.

Well, He has not changed and He wants you to experience a joy unspeakable and full-of-glory relationship with Him. (1 Peter 1:8) To please God, we must walk by faith and not doubt in His ability to complete the good work He started in you. (Philippians 1:6)

ENCOURAGE YOURSELF!

Where the Spirit of the Lord is there is freedom, Jesus has made you free to be all He has purposed you to be.

When there is no one around, learn how to Encourage yourself with the Word of God.

Submit yourselves therefore to God. Resist the devil and he will flee from you. (James 4:7)

Humble yourselves in the sight of the Lord, and He shall lift you up. (James 4:10)

Having therefore these promises, dearly beloved, let us cleanse ourselves from all filthiness of the flesh and spirit, perfecting holiness in the fear of God. (2 Corinthians 7:1)

And whosoever shall exalt himself shall be abased, and he that shall humble himself shall be exalted. (Matthew 23:12)

If any man will come after me, let him deny himself and take up his cross and follow me. (Matthew 16:24)

Likewise reckon you also yourselves to be dead indeed unto sin, but alive unto God through Jesus Christ our Lord. (Romans 6:11)

Let not sin therefore reign in your mortal (self) body that ye should obey it and the lusts thereof. (Romans 6:12)

Neither yield your members as instruments of unrighteousness unto sin, but yield yourself unto God as those that are alive from the dead and your members are instruments of righteousness unto God. (Romans 6:13)

Keep yourselves in the love of God, looking for the mercy of our Lord Jesus Christ unto eternal life. (Jude 1:21)

But, ye beloved, building up yourselves on your most holy faith, praying in the Holy Ghost. (Jude 1:20)

He that speaks in an unknown tongue <u>edifies</u> himself. (1 Corinthians 14:4)

Not that we are sufficient of ourselves to think anything as of ourselves, but our <u>sufficiency is of God</u>. (2 Corinthians 3:5)

Then Jesus answered, "The Son of Man <u>can do nothing of Himself</u> but what He sees the Father do...." (John 5:19)

I can of mine own self do nothing, as I hear, I judge; And my judgment is just because <u>I seek not mine own will</u>, but the will of the Father which hath sent me. (John 5:30)

David was a man after God's own heart, but when he was overtaken by the enemy and the men with him spoke of stoning him, he had to <u>encourage himself in the Lord</u>. Read 1 Samuel 30:1-26.

The Word of God is the answer to any circumstance and will cause you to rise above any oppressing situation.

RIGHT STANDING WITH GOD

Dear beloved,

Everyone born into this world has a question within them that must be answered before they can live a peaceful and successful life. That question is the same one God asked Adam and Eve in the Garden of Eden: Where are you? (Genesis 3:9, NKJV) They had to define their position to God since they were no longer where He had put them.

The same is true today. He wants everyone to know where they are as far as He is concerned. Are you righteous or are you a sinner? How would you respond?

We find in the Word of God that there is a difference between a righteous man and a sinner! God's law was not made for a righteous man, but for the sinners. (1 Timothy 1:9; Mark 2:17; Luke 5:32; 1 John 3:10)

When you plan a trip to go anywhere in this world, one of the first things you have to know is where you are. If I gave you a map and told you to go to Alaska, you may know your destination, but if you don't know where you are on the map, it would be very difficult to reach your goal. So it is with our standing with God. If we don't know how we stand with God, it makes it very difficult to come into His presence. This is very important! In order for a man to live peacefully and successfully, he must have a relationship with God. (Romans 5:1; 1 John 1:7)

There were men in the Bible who found out their standing with God and began to move closer after it was revealed to them. One such man was the publican who went into the Temple and, standing afar off, he said, "Be merciful to me a sinner." (Luke 18:14) After talking with God, he came out justified (made righteous). He acknowledged where he was and received God's provision to make him righteous.

Another case was Peter, when he let down one net when Jesus told him to "let down your nets." He saw his disobedience and said, "I am a sinful man, O Lord." Yet, Jesus told him, "Fear not; from now on thou shall catch men." (Luke 5:1-11) Peter then followed Jesus, after he located himself.

God spoke to King Ahab about selling himself to work wickedness in the sight of the Lord, and he very abominably followed idols. When Ahab heard these words concerning his position with God, he tore his clothes, fasted, and mourned. God said, "Because he humbled himself before me, I will not bring evil in his days." (1 Kings 21:25-29)

WHERE ARE YOU TODAY? ARE YOU RIGHTEOUS OR ARE YOU A SINNER?

Some believe they are righteous, but are deceived. Jesus spoke of them as those which justify themselves before men – but God knows your heart; for that which is highly esteemed among men is abomination in the sight of God. (Luke 16:15) Even as the Pharisee stood and prayed with himself and said, "God, I thank you that I am not as other men are, extortionist, unjust, adulterers, I fast twice a week. I give tithes of all that I possess." (Luke 18:11-12) Notice how many times he said "I". He trusted in himself that he was righteous and he despised others. (Luke 18:9)

These kinds of folks exist today. They are self-righteous. They think that because I read my Bible; I pray; I go to church; I don't smoke or drink; I try not to hurt anybody; I believe I'm just as good as anyone else. That's not what makes us righteous. (Romans 10:3)

No! It is not what you do of yourself that makes you righteous. It is what God gives to everyone who receives it through faith in the Lord Jesus Christ, trusting not in what's done, but trusting and believing in what Jesus has done for us. For with the heart man believes unto righteousness (right-standing with God). (Romans 10:10)

All men are born sinners and need someone to deliver them from their sinfulness. Christ Jesus came into the world to save sinners (1 Timothy 1:15) because all (including you and I) have sinned and sin separates us from God, (Isaiah 59:2) even as Adam and Eve hid themselves from the presence of God because of their sin. (Genesis 3:8) Jesus paid the penalty for your sins and your punishment was laid upon Him. He became your sin that you might become His righteousness. (2 Corinthians 5:21)

We need to receive this position of righteousness, which God has provided for everyone who believes in Jesus Christ. (Romans 5:15-19; Romans 3:22) Abraham believed God and it was counted unto him for righteousness. (Romans 4:3) With Jesus' death, burial, and resurrection, how much more are we counted in with faithful Abraham?

The scripture also declares that righteousness (right-standing with God) is imputed (given) if we believe on Him that raised up Jesus our Lord from the dead. (Romans 4:24) It is not your works that make you righteous. We must believe in (trust, rely on, cling to) the Lord Jesus.

All those who truly trust God confess their sins. And God is faithful and just to forgive our sins and to cleanse us from ALL unrighteousness. (1 John 1:9) The Blood of Jesus is sufficient to cleanse us from all sin, (1 John 1:7) keeping us with a clear conscience towards God and man. There is nothing that can separate us from God. (Romans 8:38-39) We are in right-standing with God continually. We do not trust in self or any other thing, but in Jesus Christ, Who is our righteousness. (1 Corinthians 1:30-31)

WE ARE RIGHTEOUS:

Isaiah 54:17	Romans 4:21-22	Romans 10:4
Romans 3:22	Romans 5:19	Romans 14:17
Romans 4:3	Romans 8:3-4	2 Corinthians 5:21

THE BLESSINGS OF RIGHTEOUSNESS:

Proverbs 11:30	tree of life
Proverbs 14:34	exalts a nation (people)
Proverbs 15:6	treasures
Proverbs 18:10	safety
Proverbs 21:21	finds life and honor
Matthew 5:10	happy when persecuted
Matthew 6:33	all things added to you
John 15:7	answered prayers
Philippians 4:13	can do all things
James 5:16	prayers avail much
1 Peter 3:12	God's watching over you
1 John 5:15	answered petitions

Section Three

Encouraging words for comfort

PRAYER

Prayer is essential for the development of our spiritual lives. When communicating with God, there is peace.

Having fellowship with God, through prayer, we make very few errors in our day-to-day activities. He that walks in the Spirit shall not fulfill the lust of the flesh. (Galatians 5:16) My heart's desire is to be in touch with God continually. I know that His ears are open unto my cry and His eyes are upon me, beholding my manner of living. (1 Peter 3:12) But, in order to have a God-like attitude in all I do, my ears must be open to His voice and my eyes must see Him through His Word, Jesus Christ.

Prayer is one of the most neglected privileges in the body of Christ and because of the lack of prayer, people lack knowledge and perish. (Hosea 4:6) There is such a thing as a second-hand religion, where people are being fed the Word of God by those who they esteem to be spiritually mature. For example, when Moses went up to the mountain to talk with God, the people heard the thundering, the great noise, and saw the lightning. They stood afar off and told Moses to speak with us and we will hear, but let not God speak with us lest we die. (Exodus 20:19) They were afraid of a direct fellowship with God.

A sin conscience will cause you to draw back from God, because of guilt of past sin and errors. But thanks be to God who has provided a way in which every man can draw near to Him. In the presence of God, there is fullness of joy. (Psalm 16:11) God wants to communicate with you today. Let us draw near with full assurance, entering into the holiest by the Blood of Jesus. (Hebrews 10:19)

Many are living in sin because they have not received their salvation. There are those who have not received the Holy Spirit because they are trying to earn Him by doing certain things. Some are wondering why they have not received from God.

God has provided for all your needs to be met. (Philippians 4:19) Still there are those who have not because they ask not. (James 4:3) Ask and it shall be given; seek and ye shall find; knock and it shall be opened unto you, for everyone that asks receives and he that seeks finds. (Matthew 7:7-8) When we ask, we must ask in faith, not wavering, (James 1:6) but believing that God is able and will perform that which He has promised. (Romans 4:21) Do not be afraid to ask God for what you need. He will do more than you ask or think. (Ephesians 3:20) For if you know how to give good gifts unto your children, how much more shall your heavenly Father give the Holy Spirit to them that ask Him? (Luke 11:13)

Whenever the devil comes to accuse, we must rely on the Blood of Jesus which makes and keeps us in right standing with God. We pray in faith, not begging and pleading with God, but in an attitude of respect and dependence on His vast supply. We learn to avail our life to the blessings, power, wisdom, and riches that God has already provided for us by His covenant with us.

Let's talk to God today!!!

Below are scriptures that give examples of different ways to pray. This list is not an exhaustive list.

PRAYER:

Matthew 6:5-15 – Jesus teaches how to pray
John 17:1-26 – Jesus prays
1 Corinthians 14:2 – pray mysteries to God
1 Corinthians 14:4 – benefit of praying in the Spirit
1 Corinthians 14:14 – your spirit praying
Ephesians 6:17-19 – praying in the Spirit
1 Timothy 2:8 – pray everywhere
Hebrews 4:16 – go boldly to God
2 Thessalonians 5:17 – pray without ceasing
1 Timothy 2:1-2 – pray for all men
Hebrews 13:18 – pray for leadership
James 5:13-18 – prayer of faith
Jude 20 – build yourself up

PRAYER FROM THE WORD:

Acts 4:24-31
Ephesians 1:15-23

Ephesians 3:14-21
Ephesians 6:19-20
Philippians 1:9-11
Colossians 1:9-11
Colossians 4:2-4
2 Thessalonians 1:11-12
2 Thessalonians 3:1-2

PRAYERS OF PETITION (ASKING):

Matthew 7:7-11
John 14:13-14
John 15:7
John 16:23-24
Ephesians 3:20
James 4:2-3

PRAYERS OF THANKSGIVING:

Ephesians 1:16
Philippians 4:6-7
Colossians 1:12
Colossians 3:15-17
1 Timothy 2:1

CONFIDENCE

We must develop and maintain our confidence in God. Therefore, my desire is to exhort all in Christ Jesus to cast not away your confidence which hath a great recompense of reward. (Hebrews 10:35) There are many things that will come against a child of God, but as soon as we recognize there is an enemy of our souls, we must build up ourselves on our most holy faith, praying in the Holy Spirit, (Jude 20) for we are to praise and glorify God in all things.

We are confident of this very thing, that He which hath begun a good work in you will perform it until the day of Jesus. (Philippians 1:6) Don't believe the devil when he tells you that you aren't anything. God has begun a good work in you. Stop looking at the problems, circumstances, and what people say about you, or even your past. God is more than able to complete that work He started in you. Be encouraged. Keep your confidence built up in God through His Word. Begin to see what God has done for you. Keep your eyes on the Word of God. He is able to do exceedingly, abundantly above all that we ask or think according to the power that works in you. (Ephesians 3:20)

Find out what is in you, so that the communication of your faith may become effective by acknowledging every good thing which is in you in Christ Jesus. (Philemon 6) We are partakers of Christ, if we hold the beginning of our confidence steadfast unto the end. (Hebrews 3:14) There is no lack in Christ and we are partakers of His divine nature. Don't forget that! Be steadfast! Don't let the devil rob you of your confidence in the Lord, for we are Christ's! Our rejoicing and hope must be in the work of Jesus Christ. Rejoicing keeps your confidence alive and active. Hope and expectation must be kept alive and active. A merry heart is good and is better than medicine. (Proverbs 15:13, 15b; Proverbs 17:22)

An example of how to deal with a lack of confidence is seen in the life of David. When in distress, David asked himself, why are you cast down, O my soul and why are you disquieted within me? Hope in God, for I shall yet praise Him who is the help of my countenance and my God. (Psalm

42:11, NKJV) David built his confidence by telling his soul to hope in God. You can do the same. (Isaiah 30:15b)

Although persecution, affliction, sickness, disease, distress, poverty, sin, and doubt comes to shake our faith, we must stand our ground and know that God has not left us or forsaken us. Those who have learned the way of victory have found out that we must do as David did in the time of trouble. For David was greatly distressed, and the people spoke of stoning him because the souls of the people were grieved. But David encouraged himself in the Lord his God. (1 Samuel 30:6) His encouragement caused him to rise above defeat, gain victory, and recover everything the enemy took from him and his people. When you rise above defeat with confidence, you will begin to believe, I am more than a conqueror through Him that loves me. I can do all things through Christ which strengthens me. (Philippians 4:13) I will make it!!

LET'S SEE WHAT THE WORD SAYS:

Isaiah 30:15b, in quietness and confidence shall be your strength.

Proverbs 33:21-26, the Lord shall be thy confidence and shall keep thy foot from being taken.

Proverbs 14:26, in the fear of the Lord is strong confidence; and His children shall have a place of refuge.

Isaiah 54:17, no weapon that is formed against thee shall prosper … their righteousness is of me.

1 John 5:4-6, who is he that overcomes the world but he that believed that Jesus is the Son of God.

1 John 5:14-15, and this is the confidence that we have in Him, that if we ask anything according to His will, He hears us, and if we KNOW that He hear us, whatsoever we ask, we KNOW that we have the petitions that we desire of Him.

2 Timothy 1:7, for God has not given us the spirit of fear, but of power, and of love, and of a sound mind.

2 Thessalonians 3:16, Now the Lord of peace Himself give you peace always by all means.

PEACE

Greetings disturbed one,

Thank God for this day of righteousness, for God is not the author of confusion, but of peace. When the devil comes with confusion, sickness, lack, or sin, I do not have to accept it. God has not given me the spirit of fear, but of power and of love and of a sound mind. (2 Timothy 1:7) Let the peace of God rule in your heart every day.

Peace remains in your heart as you love the truth. Great peace have they that love Thy law and nothing shall offend them. (Psalm 119:165) Jesus said, "My peace I leave with you, My peace I give unto you; not as the world giveth give I unto you. Let not your heart be troubled, neither let it be afraid." (John 14.27) This is the day which the Lord hath made, we will rejoice and be glad in it. (Psalm 118:24)

God has given peace. Let us let peace reign and rule. Give the Word of God first place in your life today. In communication with God, there is peace. Ask and ye shall receive, that your joy might be full. (John 16:24) When we talk to God, we are in His presence and in His presence is fullness of joy. (Psalm 16:11)

Jesus is at the right hand of the Father praying for your success on this earth. Talk to the Father and He will talk to you. Jesus said, "These things I have spoken unto you that you be not offended." (John 16:1) There is peace in talking to the Father in the name of Jesus. Don't look at the problem, look at the promise.

Let the Word of God fill you with peace that passes all understanding. (Philippians 4:7)

Matthew 5:9, Blessed are the peacemakers: for they shall be called the children of God.

Romans 2:10, But glory, honor, and peace, to every man that works good, to the Jew first, and also to the Gentile.

Romans 5:1, Therefore being justified by faith, we have peace with God through our Lord Jesus Christ....

Romans 8:6, For to be carnally minded is death; but to be spiritually minded is life and peace.

Romans 12:18, If it be possible, as much as lies in you, live peaceably with all men.

Romans 14:17, For the kingdom of God is not meat and drink; but righteousness, and peace, and joy in the Holy Ghost.

Romans 16:20b, And the God of peace shall bruise Satan under your feet shortly.

Ephesians 2:14, For he is our peace, who hath made both one, and hath broken down the middle wall of partition between us....

Colossians 1:19-20, For it pleased the Father that in him should all fullness dwell; And, having made peace through the blood of his cross, by him to reconcile all things unto himself; by him, I say, whether they be things in earth, or things in heaven.

1 Timothy 2:1-2, I exhort therefore, that, first of all, supplications, prayers, intercessions, and giving of thanks, be made for all men; For kings, and for all that are in authority; that we may lead a quiet and peaceable life in all godliness and honesty.

James 3:18, And the fruit of righteousness is sown in peace of them that make peace.

1 Peter 3:11, Let him turn away from evil and do well; Let him seek peace and pursue it.

2 Peter 3:14, Wherefore, beloved, seeing that ye look for such things, be diligent that ye may be found of him in peace, without spot, and blameless.

REST

Dear unsettled one,

Rest means to refrain from activity especially in order to recover energy. Jesus encourages us to come to Him, all who are heavy laden (overburdened with anxiety), and He will give you rest. (Matthew 11:28) Learn of Him. He is the rest you are looking for!

Many are searching for a time of quiet, a chance to escape, a place of refuge. If there is ever a time rest is being sought after, it is now. Rest is needed in our homes, our relationships, our comings and goings, in our financial obligations, and the list can go on. (Isaiah 30:15b)

God declares through the Apostle Paul that there remains a rest to the people of God. We enter into that rest as we cease from our own works. As we let go of our way of doing what we do and let God show us a new way to get done what He desires. (Hebrews 4:8-11) We have to be taught how to do things His way.

Moses, the great leader of Israel, had to listen to his father-in-law, Jethro, when it came to sharing leadership responsibilities with other leaders in the nation. (Exodus 18:13-26) He had to rest and trust Jethro's judgment.

When Jesus fed the multitude in the wilderness, they had to obey His disciples' directions to sit in groups where they could rest and be fed. The women and children also had to rest. (Mark 6:31)

As the good Shepherd the Lord makes His sheep (His chosen ones) to lie down in green pastures; He leads them beside the still waters and restores their soul (mind, will, and emotions). (Psalm 23:2-3)

The man, with mental illness, was sitting at the feet of Jesus, clothed and in his right mind after the evil spirit was driven out from him and he rested. (Luke 8:35)

As Martha toiled in the kitchen, Mary rested at Jesus' feet to receive a word for the journey that was yet to come. (Luke 10:38-42)

God has to give us rest from the struggles of this life or life would overtake us. God, Himself, rested after He created the universe in six days. On the seventh day He rested and He said His works were very good. (Exodus 20:8-11)

So what is it you need rest from?

Many do not find rest because they feel there is no need to honor and serve God. There is no eternal rest outside of the true and living God. He made His rest available to man through the Prince of Peace, Jesus Christ. Jesus is waiting to receive you just as you are. You do not have to earn brownie points or accumulate any amount of works or good deeds. He has already paid the price for the rest you are looking for.

Please come unto Him all who are weary and burdened with care and He will give you rest. You will begin to learn of Him for His yoke is easy and His burden is light.

Take the first step and Rest in God, His way!

STRENGTH

Whenever you are weak,

The strength of God is an inward strength. When your heart is strengthened, it can receive. Follow the Word of God and abide in it, thus, you can endure the temptations and persecutions of life.

Wait on the Lord: be of good courage, and He shall strengthen your heart: Wait, I say, on the Lord. (Psalm 27:14)

The Lord is my strength and my shield; my heart trusted in Him and I am helped. Therefore my heart greatly rejoices and with my song will I praise Him. The Lord is my strength and He is the saving strength of His anointed. (Psalm 28:7-8)

The Lord will give strength unto His people; the Lord will bless His people with peace. (Psalm 29:11)

Be of good courage, and He shall strengthen your heart, all that hope in the Lord. (Psalm 31:24)

…the salvation of the righteous is of the LORD: He is their strength in the time of trouble. (Psalm 37:39)

When God spoke to Paul, he received the strength he needed to endure. Paul prayed that God would grant the church at Ephesus, according to the riches of His glory, to be strengthened with might by His Spirit in the inner man. (Ephesians 3:16)

No matter what state you find yourself in, God wants you to learn to draw from the wells of living water and receive inner strength. (Proverbs 16:22; Proverbs 18:4) He says that His strength is made perfect in weakness. (2 Corinthians 12:9) When you are at your lowest point and you don't know what to do, in your weakness, draw from God's strength.

When Paul was forsaken, the Lord stood with him. No man stood with me, but all men forsook me; Notwithstanding the Lord stood with me and

31

strengthened me; that by me the preaching might be fully known, and that all the Gentiles might hear; and I was delivered out of the mouth of the lion. (2 Timothy 4:16-17)

Be still and know that I am God.... Psalm 46:10

Section Four

Encouraging words for forgiveness

GOD FORGIVES MAN

God's first act of forgiveness toward man was shown when Adam and Eve disobeyed and listened to the serpent who said that God was holding out on them. (Genesis 3:5)

Wherefore, as by one man sin entered into the world, and death by sin, and so death passed upon all men, for that all have sinned. (Romans 5:12)

There had to be a way for man to be redeemed back to God. God had planned for Jesus to die for the sins of the whole world way before Adam and Eve sinned. Jesus' blood that was shed on Calvary's tree is the only thing that has the power to forgive mankind and to cleanse all from the power of sin.

Jesus was the perfect example of God's forgiveness toward man. An adulterous woman, caught in the very act, was brought to Jesus. When her accusers could not throw the first stone because of their guilt, Jesus told her, "Neither do I condemn thee." The accusers went away convicted by their own conscience. Jesus reassured the woman that He did not condemn her, but she should go and sin no more. (John 8:3-11)

Jesus told the man sick of the palsy, "Son, be of good cheer; thy sins be forgiven thee." (Matthew 9:2)

Although the scribes, Pharisees, and rulers criticized Jesus for forgiving sins, He asked them what was easier to say, take up the bed and walk or to forgive sins. To Jesus they are one in the same because He came to earth to set men free from the bondage of sin.

Mankind must receive Christ's forgiveness for them to live free.

God so loved the world that He gave His only begotten Son, that whosoever believes in Him (Jesus) should not perish, but have everlasting life. (John 3:16)

Are you a whosoever? Then God is directing His love to you. Choose to believe in His love.

God sent not His Son into the world to condemn the world, but that the world through Him might be saved. (John 3:17)

MEN FORGIVE MEN

If your brother shall trespass against thee, go and tell him his fault between you and him alone; if he shall hear you, you have gained your brother. (Matthew 18:15)

Peter asked, "Lord, how often shall my brother sin against me, and I forgive him? Till seven times?" Jesus said unto him, "I say not unto thee, Up to seven times: but, up to seventy times seven." (Matthew 18:21-22)

When we harbor unforgiveness and don't confirm our love, it causes others to be swallowed up with sorrow and sometimes hardens them to God's Love.

It is not natural for man to forgive when he has been hurt or unjustly treated. Instead we want an eye for an eye or a tooth for a tooth, but we must choose to let the mind of Christ be in us and do as He commands.

Jesus told his disciples to love your enemies, bless them that curse you, do good to them that hate you, pray for them which despitefully use you, and persecute you; that ye may be the children of your Father which is in heaven; For He makes His sun to rise on the evil and on the good, and sends rain on the just and on the unjust. (Matthew 5:44-45)

One of the greatest wounds in life is to be let down by someone in a leadership position, especially in ministry. In the book of Luke we read the story of the religious leaders who failed to reach out to someone in need. But when a Samaritan traveler was moved with compassion, he saw the wounded and, with no thought of reward, helped him to a place of rest to begin to heal. The Samaritan covered the expenses, told the inn keeper that he would return, and if there was not enough, he would take care of it upon his return. As the wounded healed, he no doubt had to forgive those who refused to help him when he was down, so his healing could begin. (Luke 10:31-32)

We must guard our heart from thoughts that lead to unforgiveness. 1 Samuel 18:28 tells of a process Saul went through that developed unforgiveness in his heart toward David. The process started when Saul became jealous of David. The women praised David's ten thousand victories compared to Saul's thousand. His view of David became distorted to the degree of trying to kill David, who eventually had to run for his life. Some might say this was no big deal; however, we read where Saul spent the rest of his life trying to hunt David. Anger began to rest in Saul. (Ecclesiastes 7:9) The songs of praise he once desired to bring him peace were now traded for words that caused affliction and turmoil, but only in Saul. (Proverbs 10:18)

David had opportunity to kill Saul a couple times, but he would not raise his hand against the Lord's anointed. (1 Samuel 26:9, 11, 23) David was innocent of the thoughts and hatred Saul had toward him, but Saul pursued without a cause. One evil thought turned into a lifetime pursuit for someone who was only after knowing the heart of God. With all the years of running, David chose to forgive Saul.

Mankind has a choice to forgive. Forgiveness for another can only happen when one has received forgiveness. Let God's forgiveness embrace your life. When you know you are forgiven, you will also be willing to forgive others.

WORDS TO THINK ABOUT:

Joseph's brothers asked him to forgive them. (Genesis 50:17)

The spirit of a man will sustain his infirmity, but a wounded spirit who can bear? (Proverbs 18:14)

The words of a talebearer are as wounds, and they go down into the innermost parts of the belly. (Proverbs 26:22)

And one shall say unto him, what are these wounds in thy hands? Then he shall answer those with which I was wounded in the house of my friends. (Zechariah 13:6)

And be ye kind one to another, tender-hearted, forgiving one another, even as God for Christ's sake hath forgiven you. (Mark 4:32)

And when ye stand praying; forgive, if ye have aught against any, that your Father also which is in heaven may forgive you your trespasses. But if ye do not forgive, neither will your Father which is in heaven forgive your transgressions. (Mark 11:25-26)

To whom little is forgiven, the same loves little. (Luke 7:47)

Forbearing one another, and forgiving one another; if any man has a quarrel against any; even as Christ forgave you, so also do ye. (Ephesians 4:32)

Finally, brothers and sisters, whatever is true, whatever is noble, whatever is right, whatever is pure, whatever is lovely, whatever is admirable; if anything is excellent or praiseworthy, think about such things. (Philippians 4:8, NIV)

FORGIVENESS

Vengeance is one of the main hindrances that causes men and women to harden their hearts and not forgive. It does not matter how spiritual you are, when someone trespasses against you, there is a force telling you to judge that which has been done according to the way you were treated; we suffer grief when we are wrongfully treated.

When we are mistreated, sometimes we get angry. A decision must be made as to whether one should forgive or seek some means by which one can get revenge. But God said, "Rather give place to wrath. Vengeance is mine; I will repay." (Romans 12:19) All our wrath and anger is to be put away from us. How? Let us see!

We can feel the hurt when someone does us wrong. Even in heaven there are those who were slain for the Word of God and the testimony that they held and they cry with a loud voice saying, how long, O Lord, Holy and True, does Thou not judge and avenge our blood on them that dwell in the earth? And white robes were given unto every one of them that they should rest yet for a little season. (Revelation 6:10-11) We cry out, sometimes, wanting to have justice done on our behalf.

Forgiveness is a releasing of another from your own judgment. We must realize that God has a day of wrath and revelation of His righteous judgment. (Romans 2:5) When you do not forgive, you are not at rest. As they cried under the altar, God gave them righteousness (robes) that they might rest.

We must see the goodness of God in our life in order to forgive others. When we truly see God dealing justly with us, it doesn't matter who is against us. If God is for us, who can be against us? (Romans 8:31)

We must know our standing with God. Even as David said that I will take heed to my ways that I sin not with my tongue while the wicked is before me. Lord, make me to know my end and the measure of my days. (Psalm 39:1, 4) When he went into the sanctuary, he understood that the wicked were standing in a slippery position. It would be better for them to have a millstone around their necks and to be cast into the sea. (Mark 9:42) So, it's God's goodness that is keeping the wicked alive and giving them a chance to repent. It is the goodness of God that leads men to repentance. (Romans 2:4)

Your goodness from God to others will lead others to repentance. Christ, who for the joy that was set before Him, endured the cross, despising the shame and is set down on the right hand of God. (Hebrews 12:2)

We love Him because He first loved us! (1 John 4:19) While we were yet sinners, Christ died for us. (Romans 5:8) Now He lives in and through us! Praise God!

There was a man who owed his master a large debt, which amounted to about nine million dollars. When the master came to him for payment, the servant fell at his master's feet and begged for mercy. The master forgave his entire debt. But in time, someone owed the same servant about twenty-eight dollars and his fellow servant asked the servant for mercy. Angrily, the servant grabbed him by the neck, choked him and put him in prison until all was paid. Apparently the servant forgot the goodness that was shown to him. (Matthew 18:22-35)

Even so, as children of God, we must forgive even as God, for Christ's sake, has forgiven us. (Ephesians 4:32) Because Jesus is good, are we able to forgive. When forgiveness becomes real to us then are we able to forgive, and as we experience God's forgiveness then we can let others know they can experience His forgiveness as well.

POWER IN THE BLOOD

Jesus suffered for me so I could be sanctified (cleansed) by His blood.

Without His blood, my sins could not be erased.

I have been purchased with His blood.

I have been brought back to God with Jesus' blood and I am forgiven.

I believe in the cleansing power of Jesus' blood, I get mercy and I am now righteous.

I draw near to the Father because of Jesus' blood.

All things are connected because of the blood.

A new covenant (agreement) has been made by Jesus' blood and as often as I drink of it (symbolically through communion) I am remembering what Christ has done for me.

During communion I partake of the body and blood of the Lamb of God, therefore I am in Jesus and He is in me.

This covenant (agreement) in His blood is everlasting.

SCRIPTURES AS THEY APPEAR:

Hebrews 13:12	1 John 1:7	Revelation 1:5
Acts 20:28	Colossians 1:14	1 Peter 1:19
Hebrews 9:14	Hebrews 10:19	Colossians 1:20
1 Corinthians 11:25	Hebrews 13:20	

A DREAM

I had a dream one night about unforgiveness. In this dream, I was walking out of a church service. There were two men in front of me. I heard one say to the other, "I've been wanting to tell you something, and the Lord has told me it's time for me to speak. Please examine yourself to see if there is anyone you are holding a grudge against. If you are, you'd better let that thing go and forgive them."

The young man responded, "I don't hate anybody. I love everybody."

The first man said, "Alright, if you don't let that thing go, it's going to catch up with you. You'd better forgive them."

The young man replied again, "I don't hate anybody. I love everybody."

The dream changed and I began to walk down a flight of stairs. At the bottom of the stairs a dingy gray wolf was sitting. I had to squeeze by it quietly. I turned when I heard a lot of noise.

When I looked up, the young man was coming down the stairs behind me. As I watched him, I said to myself, "He shouldn't come down the stairs with all that noise, he'll provoke the wolf!" Sure enough, the wolf was provoked and took off after him.

The scene changed again and I was on a balcony. As I looked down, I could see the wolf continuing to chase the young man. As they passed under the balcony, I smelled a horrible odor.

A woman's voice spoke in my left ear and said, "That cancer surely smells."

I said, "It surely does smell, but that's not a cancer; that's a wolf."

The scene changed again and there was an old woman and the young man was chasing the wolf. The wolf passed under me again and that smell came into my nostrils.

Just as before, I heard the voice say, "That cancer surely smells."

I said again, "It surely does smell, but that's not a cancer; that's a wolf."

As the woman and the young man chased the wolf, they finally cornered him and began to beat him viciously. The wolf's features began to change, first into a man, then into a hideous figure.

I woke up and said, "God! What does this dream mean?" He said, "Unforgiveness causes cancer."

There are many physical ailments that can be traced directly to unforgiveness. We need to keep ourselves free from any unclean thoughts that will hinder us from loving the way Jesus has said we are to love. (John 15:12)

Colossians 3:13b says that if any man have a quarrel against any; even as Christ forgave you, so also do ye.

It is satan who brings those unclean thoughts to our minds. But his babblings are profane and we should shun them because they will eat like a canker (cancer). (2 Timothy 2:16) If we are children of God, God has shed His love abroad in our hearts. A decision must be made on the part of the believer: I'm going to let the love of God flow through me. We can't stop those unclean thoughts that tell us to hate someone from coming to us, but we can deal with them when they come so they will not affect our hearts. (Philippians 4:8, 9, 13; 1 John 1:7-9)

If we miss it and let satan plant thoughts in our minds against someone, then to deal with it, we must receive the blood of Jesus to cleanse it out of our system. It takes the blood to cleanse us from sin. (1 John 1:7-9) It takes the Word to keep us from sin. (Psalm 119:11)

The Bible tells us to cast down imaginations. (1 Corinthians 10:5) By the Word of God, our minds and thoughts are brought into the obedience of Christ, and we can cast the thoughts of satan down. How? By speaking the Word of God as Jesus did; by saying, "It is written." (Matthew 4:4, 7, 10)

And this is His commandment, that we should believe
on the name of His Son, Jesus Christ, and love one
another, as He gave us commandment.
1 John 3:23

Section Five

Encouraging words for faith in God

DRAW NEAR TO GOD

Draw near to Him and He will draw near to you.
God wants your heart to be at peace.
God wants your heart to be at rest.
Trust Him. Trust Him. Trust Him.
He made you. He knows all about you.
Run to Him. Cleave to Him.
He is not so far away that He cannot be touched with the feelings of your
infirmities.
But your feelings will not move Him.
He has given you a measure of faith.
Let it grow. Let it grow. Let it grow.
He has given you faith the size of a mustard seed.
God's mustard seed has the ability to produce a mighty tree with deep
roots and strong branches.
Be that tree of righteousness. Produce seed-bearing fruit.
That fruit will multiply in the lives of those who benefit from your fruit.
Do not despise the pruning times.
Let all the dead branches and withered leaves fall to the ground.
Do not hold onto them. Let them fall.
More fruit is produced as the deadness is cut off.
Let your fruit grow to maturity.
Be on guard to not let the fruit be picked before it is ripe.
Grow, blossom, and produce.
It is a continuous cycle that brings Glory to God.
God is not a God that is a far off.
Draw near to Him and He will draw near to you.

UNDERSTAND GOD

Most precious jewel,

Be ye not unwise, but understanding what the will of the Lord is. (Ephesians 5:17) It has been said that we cannot understand God. THAT IS NOT TRUE!! God gives us understanding that we may know Him. Many do not enjoy God's best because they do not understand God and His will for them. Where does understanding come from? How do we get it? What happens to you when you do not have understanding? What happens when you receive understanding and act upon it? Let's explore this by answering four important questions.

Question One: Where does understanding come from?

Proverbs 2:6 declares that the Lord gives wisdom; out of His mouth cometh knowledge and understanding. Understanding comes from God. Also, 1 John 5:20 says the Son of God is come and hath given us an understanding, that we may know Him that is true, and we are in Him that is true, even in His Son Jesus Christ. Spiritual understanding comes from God.

When Daniel needed understanding and the interpretation for the king's dreams, he sought God. When he received the meaning, he said, "Blessed be the name of God forever and ever; for wisdom and might are His. He gives wisdom unto the wise, and knowledge to them that know understanding. He reveals the deep and secret things...." (Daniel 2:20-22) So if you lack understanding in any matter, you can see from the Word of God that God is the source of true spiritual understanding.

Question Two: How do we receive understanding?

Some people are hoping that one day they will awaken and understanding will drop on them. Before I knew God, I used to take the Bible and put it on my chest, hoping that the words would somehow enter into me. It didn't work!

God has a very simple way for us to receive the understanding that we need. You have to want to understand! God will not force His wisdom and understanding upon you. But you will have to apply your heart to understanding; yes, cry after knowledge and lift up thy voice for understanding; if thou seek her as silver and search for her as for hid treasures, then shalt you understand the fear of the Lord and find the knowledge of God. (Proverbs 2:2-5) Yes, we must search, seek, and open our hearts to understanding.

Question Three: What will happen to you if you don't have God's understanding?

God wants His Word to be shared across earth. He desires that the Word take root in the lives of men and women. When anyone hears the Word of the kingdom and understands it not, then comes the wicked one (devil) and takes away the Word out of their hearts, lest they should believe and be saved. (Matthew 13:19; Luke 8:12) That is the way satan wants to keep us, ignorant of God's Word; but God wants us to have an understanding. My people are destroyed for lack of knowledge. (Hosea 4:6) Misunderstandings of God's will for your life will cause you to err and set you on a course in life that is not God's best for you. (Matthew 22:29)

Question Four: What happens when a person receives and acts on God's understanding?

The Word of God says that discretion shall preserve them, understanding shall keep them. (Proverbs 2:11) Yes, understanding will keep you from evil and many things that people are being overtaken by. Understanding will deliver you from the evil man and from those who speak forward things. (Proverbs 2:12) When you have understanding, the Bible declares you will be happy. (Proverbs 3:13) You will gain when you understand. (Proverbs 3:14) You receive life with understanding. (Proverbs 3:18) When you exalt understanding in your life, it will promote you. Yes, it will also bring you to honor; understanding shall give your head an ornament of grace, a crown of glory will you get. (Proverbs 4:8-9)

Here are just a few more benefits when there is understanding:

1. You will receive strength. (Proverbs 8:14)

2. Your lifestyle will line up with understanding. (Joshua 1:8)

3. If you are a leader, you will direct and rule people well. (Proverbs 8:15-16)

4. You will receive durable riches. (Proverbs 8:18, 21)

5. You will be all right with God. (Proverbs 2:9)

I encourage everyone to seek the Lord. Seek to understand Him, for in knowing Him, you have all the answers that you need. (2 Timothy 2:17)

Let not the wise man glory in his wisdom, neither let the mighty man glory in his might; let not the rich man glory in his riches. But let him that glories glory in this that he understands and knows Me (Jesus), that I am the Lord which exercises loving kindness, judgment, and righteousness in the earth; for in these things I delight, said the Lord. (Jeremiah 9:23, 24)

MADE BY GOD

Follow Me and I will make you...

The prodigal son went to his father and said, Father, give me. (Luke 15:12) He took his inheritance and went to a faraway country. After much partying and vicarious living, his friends and his financial position changed. For the first time he had to pay attention to what was going on around him. When he hit rock bottom, his attitude became sorrowful. After a while, he came to himself, returned home and said, Father, make me. (Luke 15:19) The prodigal son had grown up and realized that his father's love surpassed any adventure that he could have on earth. The prodigal son and the eldest brother realized the truth spoken by the father, "...son, thou art ever with me and all that I have is yours." (Luke 15:31; Romans 15:31)

In Matthew 7:7-11 Jesus told us how anxious the Father is to give us good gifts. This should cause you to realize it's your Heavenly Father's good pleasure to give you the Kingdom of God. God is not holding out on you. As we mature in Him and are ever before His presence, we are able to receive and walk in His provision for us. God has (past tense, already done) blessed us with all spiritual blessing in heavenly places in Christ Jesus. (Ephesians 1:3)

There must be a 'making' process when we deal with God and when God deals with us. We need not be like the elder or the younger brother; for one asked his father amiss or in the wrong way to consume upon his lust and the elder did not have because he did not ask his father. (James 4:2-3)

When we allow God to 'make' us, then our desires begin to come in line with His desire. We become mature in Him and our confidence is that He has the best plan in mind for us. This is our confidence that we have in Him that if we ask any thing according to His will, he hears us: And if we know that He hears us, whatsoever we ask, we know that we have the petitions that we desire of Him. (1 John 5:14-15)

When our will and desires are yielded to God, He is able to impart His thoughts and plans into our lives. We must allow God to 'make' us. We do this by following the example of the Lord Jesus. Follow me and I will make you. (Matthew 4:19) His making is not a forcing of His will upon you, but a continual molding, changing, teaching, and training of your spirit, soul, and body to conform to the image of God's Son. (Romans 8:29) The change takes place as we continually behold, as in a glass (mirror) the glory of the Lord and are changed into the same image from glory to glory, even as by the Spirit of the Lord. (2 Corinthians 3:18) The inward man is renewed day by day as we surrender to the creative hand of the master builder. (2 Corinthians 4:16)

> For you, Lord, have made me glad through your work;
> I will triumph in the works of your hands.
> Psalm 92:4

THE WORD OF GOD

Dear Heir of God,

When a farmer plants his crops, he rises day by day and cannot see the plant growing, but in time there is first the blade, then the stalk, then the fruit. So it is with the life of the seed (Word) God has placed in our hearts. Day by day we rise up to walk in the newness of life, that we might fulfill the course set before us. We may not see the results immediately, but if we continue in faith, we will see the fruit of our labor; for he that plows should plow in hope, and he that threshes in hope should be partaker of his hope. (1 Corinthians 9:10)

The heart of man is very precious. It is like the soil of the earth. Whatever a man receives into his heart goes through a process of growth and it actually produces and multiplies, whether good or evil.

If a thought of destruction comes into your mind and settles in your heart, eventually it will produce an outward manifestation of something being destroyed. They conceive mischief and bring forth iniquity. (Isaiah 59:4, 13) This is an all too familiar story for the times we live in. When tragedy strikes, the phrase "he or she was a good person" always seems to surface. In contrast, man looks on the outward appearance, but God looks at the heart. (1 Samuel 16:7)

Subsequently, how much more life is in the Word of God? If a man will receive the living Word of God in his heart and let it grow in his life, as the seed grows, he will not only be changed into the likeness of God; but the renewed life will impart life to those who will receive life. There will be a renewed thought process and manner of living. (Romans 12:2)

So if you've received God's Word, don't worry about how it's going to produce in your life. Just continue to read it, speak it, and most of all, live by it because it shall produce. One waters, one plants, but God gives the increase. God watches over His Word to perform it. Yes, God's Word will grow and multiply. (Acts 12:24)

Meditate on the Word below and see your faith begin to grow:

Psalm 119:9, 11, 15, 105, 130
Proverbs 2:1-9
Proverbs 12:15
Proverbs 30:5
John 1:1
John 15:3-7
Acts 20:32
Hebrews 4:12
Revelations 19:13b

Section Six

Encouraging words for personal relations

WHO ARE YOU LISTENING TO?

There are many voices and each has a specific sound.

WHO ARE YOU LISTENING TO?

Words can have a positive or a negative effect on the way you live. Lot lived in Sodom and Gomorrah where he saw and heard the wickedness of the people and it vexed his righteous soul. (2 Peter 2:7) Daily he struggled to listen for God instead of the lies and lifestyles that surrounded him.

Adam and Eve were created perfect and there was no sin inside of them. But, when Eve heard the voice of the serpent and received his words, her thoughts became corrupt. (2 Corinthians 11:3) Adam, who was standing with her, yielded to Eve's words (Genesis 3:17) which caused him to rebel against God.

WHO ARE YOU LISTENING TO?

God asked Adam, Who told you that you were naked? We must yield our ears to God. If we stop listening for instructions, that will cause us to err from the word of knowledge. (Proverbs 19:27) For the Lord gives wisdom; out of his mouth comes knowledge and understanding. (Proverbs 2:6)

Our bodies are made where they are motivated and governed by words. (James 3:2) God originally intended for man to live by every word that proceeds out of His mouth. (Matthew 4:4) In the physical sense, our physical heart pumps, giving blood to every portion of our bodies. So it is with the spiritual make-up of our being. The center of our beings (spirit) sends out messages to every portion of our body to govern it. Out of the heart flows the issues of life. (Proverbs 4:23) If my heart is full of God's word, then my body will be governed by God's word. Hebrews 10:16 says, If the enemy fills your heart with his words, you will begin to do as he did.

I watched a program that showed how a person was hypnotized. It was demonstrated that by suggestion, a person could believe the pencil in their hand was on fire, even though it wasn't. There are many suggestions in the world. The key is whether or not you choose to believe the suggestion.

As you read these words, realize that when you are tempted to sin, it is not just you alone. There are actual evil forces that are trying to lead you to rebel against God. Paul said that whenever he did something he didn't want to do, it was not he that did it, but sin dwelling with him. (Romans 7:17) You do not have to let sin rule in your body. The Spirit of God lives within you and He will show you how to overcome any temptation. But you have to make a choice: blessing or cursing, life or death, therefore, Choose Life! (Deuteronomy 30:19)

When lucifer sinned against God, no one forced him. No one tempted him; he chose to rebel against God. (John 8:44; Isaiah 14:12-13) One third of the angels listened to him and sinned against God. Adam and Eve listened to satan (Genesis 3) and sinned against God. All throughout man's history, there has been a battle in the mind to discern between God's thoughts or the devil's thoughts. For this reason we must pray or we will be overtaken by temptation.

I have met many people who are vexed or tormented in their minds by thoughts. Worry seems to dominate their entire life. It is important to listen to the voice of God; this is the only way to truly live a healthy, peaceful, and prosperous life.

When concerned about health, God sent his word and healed (Psalm 107:20; Luke 7:7); concerning righteousness, it is by our words that we are justified, or made right (Matthew 12:34-37; Romans 10:10); concerning our daily needs (Matthew 6:33; Philippians 4:19); concerning peace (John 14:27; John 16:33; Ephesians 2:14); we are partakers of God's divine nature by His word and precious promises. (2 Peter 1:4; James 1:18)

It is important to know who you are listening to because evil words produce just as the seed of man reproduces. Whenever our desire is toward evil words, they will produce sin, unrighteousness, or death. The scripture declares that when lust has conceived, it brings forth sin. (James 1:13-15) Isaiah 59:13 lets us know we conceive evil words in our hearts first. If we let evil words into our system, they will begin to corrupt our minds and our whole being will be affected. Yes, there are words that eat just like cancer. (2 Timothy 2:16-17) They will increase to more ungodliness.

We must guard our ears from the words of satan. We have a built-in monitor; our ears try words as the mouth tastes meat. (Job 34:2-4) We taste food to determine whether or not we're going to eat it. If it doesn't taste good then we won't eat. The same with words, we have the choice to let evil thoughts into our being or reject them. Therefore, cast down imaginations and every high thing that exalts itself against the knowledge of God and bring every thought captive to the obedience of Christ. (2 Corinthians 10:4-5)

Subsequently, we must be encouraged! All who have ears to hear, give attention to reading, to exhortation, and to doctrine or teaching; when you do this, you will be able to save yourself and those who hear you. (1 Timothy 4:13, 16)

Rise up and give ear to the word of God as HE speaks to your heart!

GOD'S WORD...

Is very near (Deuteronomy 30:14) Heals (Psalm 107:20)
Is settled in Heaven (Psalm 119:89) Gives light (Psalm 119:130)
Is pure (Proverbs 30:5) Has power (Ecclesiastes 8:4a)
Produces life (John 6:63) Is truth (John 17:17)
Is quick and powerful (Hebrews 4:12) Endures forever (1 Peter 1:25a)

Examine yourself: **Who Are You Listening To?**

RETURNING TO GOD

Hello loved one,

Does it seem as though you cannot feel God's presence anymore? Many of God's children are in a position where they have grown cold toward God. Things that used to cause them to rejoice have no effect on them. What has happened??? Perhaps there is a need to return to God.

There are different degrees in backsliding. I thank God that in the past, whenever I slipped into a degree of backsliding, God delivered me and gave me an answer so I could return to Him.

There were actions and reactions that would let me know when I needed to be closer to God. One sign was the insensitivity to the needs or desires of other people. Instead of taking time to listen and pray with them, I could say yes, I will pray, but then forget all about it. A second sign was when I easily complained, was critical or easily offended. I was wearing my feelings on my sleeve. Yet another sign was when my Bible reading was put on the back burner and time was not made to talk to God often. With me not talking to God often, there was a decrease in my witnessing to others about the goodness of God. When these things occur, you can be sure something is wrong. Let us lay aside every weight and the sin which doth so easily ensnare us, and let us run with endurance the race that was set before us. (Hebrews 12:1b, NKJV)

Return unto the Lord thy God, for thou hast fallen by thine iniquity. Take with you words and turn to the Lord: say unto Him, Take away all iniquity and receive us graciously, so will we render the calves of our lips. (Hosea 14:1-2)

When I realized I had fallen away, to be restored, I had to come to God and confess my sins. He is faithful and just to forgive my sins and to cleanse me from all unrighteousness. (1 John 1:9) As God forgave, I had to believe that I was forgiven because God's Word says He will forgive. In confessing my sins, I had to forgive those who trespassed against me, then make the decision to follow peace with all men. I had to be diligent and not allow a root of bitterness to spring up, trouble me, and cause me to be defiled. (Hebrews 12:14-15) I could not listen to what people said or look too long at what was done to me. I had to keep looking unto JESUS, the author and finisher of my faith. (Hebrews 12:2)

After confession and receiving forgiveness I had to live a life that demonstrated Jesus and His Word being alive in my life. My confession is made unto salvation (daily deliverance) and I overcome the devil by the word of my testimony. Jesus said I am the salt of the earth and I am a light in this world. Whatever Jesus says I am, I begin to say it. If I say I am weak and can't make it, I will remain weak. The scripture says, let the weak say, I AM STRONG! (Joel 3:10)

So, hold fast the form of sound words, which thou hast heard of me (Paul) in faith and love which is in Christ Jesus. (2 Timothy 1:13) Fight the good fight of faith. Lay hold on eternal life where unto thou art called and hast professed (confessed) a good profession before many witnesses. (2 Timothy 6:12) Knowing we are forgiven and justified, we must exhort one another daily while it is called today, lest any of us be hardened through the deceitfulness of sin. (Hebrews 3:13) Confession is made unto salvation.

Finally, to maintain victory is to love not my life until death. We overcome the devil by the Blood of the Lamb and by the word of our testimony and we love not our lives unto the death. (Revelation 12:11) Abraham, our father of Faith, was not weak in faith; and considered not his own body, now dead, when he was about an hundred years old, neither the deadness of Sarah's womb. He staggered not at the promise of God through unbelief; but was strong in faith, giving glory to God. (Romans 4:19-25)

Praise God! Fight the good fight of Faith! (1 Timothy 6:12) In Returning to God, don't consider your body, circumstances, or problems. Consider JESUS, for what He has promised, He is able to perform. He is the author and finisher of our faith. Have Faith in God. Beware, brethren, lest there be in any of you an evil heart of unbelief in departing from the living God. (Hebrews 3:12, NKJV) Faith is the key. Without faith it is impossible to please God. (Hebrews 6:11)

Returning to God is a process. Be patient as the Holy Spirit reconciles you to God. The scriptures below will strengthen the process.

Psalm 107:20, He sent his word, and healed them, and delivered them from their destructions.

Psalm 119:11, Thy word have I hid in mine heart, that I might not sin against thee.

Psalm 119:105, Thy word is a lamp unto my feet, and a light unto my path.

John 2:5b, …Whatsoever he says unto you, do it.

John 4:34, Jesus says unto them, my meat is to do the will of him that sent me, and to finish his work.

Philippians 4:9, Those things, which ye have both learned, and received, and heard, and seen in me, do: and the God of peace shall be with you.

Colossians 3:23, And whatsoever ye do, do it heartily, as to the Lord, and not unto men.

Hebrews 4:12, For the word of God is quick, and powerful, and sharper than any two-edged sword, piercing even to the dividing asunder of soul and spirit, and of the joints and marrow, and is a discerner of the thoughts and intents of the heart.

Be a doer of the word, not a hearer only, deceiving only yourselves. (James 1:22)

STANDING ALONE

To my dear friend,

When incarcerated, there is isolation that takes place in your life. You are cut off from having an active relationship with friends, family, and the outside world. How does a person deal with isolation in an isolated place?

A decision has to be made. We can choose to go into solitude and let circumstances force us to be alone. Or we can do as Paul declared that at my first answer no man stood with me, but all men forsook me; the Lord stood with me and strengthened me. (2 Timothy 4:16-17) Yes! Many times when a person is placed in prison, people forsake him. Women divorce their husbands or husbands divorce their wives. Many prisoners do not hear anything from their family or before jail time friends and acquaintances.

We must learn to stand alone at times. As Jesus went to a mountain to pray, He continued all night in talking to God. (Luke 6:12) In the morning, rising up early, He went out and departed into a solitary (alone) place and there prayed. If you find yourself in a solitary place, PRAY. As we learn how to stand alone with God, it will help us to stand alone among men. We must recognize that God is with us. "Behold the hour comes, that you shall be scattered, every man to his own and shall leave Me alone, and yet I am not alone because the Father is with Me." (John 16:32) Jesus was left alone, yet He was not alone.

You may feel like you are all alone today, that others have forsaken you, but I encourage you to use this time to learn how to stand alone. As God said, "Be still and know that I am God." (Psalm 46:10) Use this time to allow God to search your heart and reveal what is really working in you, not just that which is evil, but that which is good, that the sharing of your faith may become effective by the acknowledging of every good thing which is in you in Christ Jesus. (Philemon 6, NKJV)

Yes! In the times of solitude you have an opportunity to see more clearly. Many times the hustle and bustle of this busy world clouds the real issues of life. Jesus told the disciples, when feeding the multitude, to make the men sit down. In order to feed them, they were told they had to sit down. In Psalm 23 David said that his Shepherd makes me to lie down in green pastures; He leads me beside the still waters. He restores my soul. When the process of restoration begins there will be a revealing of the deep things of God. (1 Corinthians 2:10)

Many times we don't want to be still because we may have to face truths about ourselves. Thus says the Lord God, the Holy One of Israel; in returning and rest shall ye be saved; in quietness and in confidence shall be your strength, but ye would not. (Isaiah 30:15-16) God desires us to be still before Him so He can renew our strength. We do not want to be like the nations of Israel in verse 10 of the same chapter of Isaiah. We don't want to run away from God, we always want to run to Him. We have many distractions to avoid quietness. We turn on the TV, computer, or cell phone. We use drugs, alcohol or sedatives. We live in denial by blaming others for our misfortunes, thereby not really looking at our motives and intentions.

An inmate sent me this letter and I would like to share a portion of his discovery:

> "I hadn't realized that my greatest fear in life was me and that I have been running from and not wanting to confront that person I saw in the mirror because of the emotional pain I felt inside. All the emotional baggage I packaged up over the years finally came to a point of unbearable weight on my mind when facing these feelings was my only choice. Even before I came to prison, I had busied myself by going through the motions of healing, but not confronting what needed to be healed – me. If anything, I know I may never have this time again in my life to learn about myself and who I am, so I had to take this opportunity and use it wisely. I started reading, journaling, listening to tapes, talking, or anything that would help me get in touch with myself. I learned about self-esteem, anger, depression, forgiveness, prayer, childhood, asking for support, love relationships, and communication. As I learned, I couldn't help but have long-dormant, unresolved feelings come to the surface and beat at my mind's door. It was uncorking the bottle and

confronting that baggage that started my healing and allowed me to see clearly for the first time in my life. What I forced myself to feel and deal with was truly painful. I don't ever want to experience it again. I had become my own worst enemy by not confronting my emotions and burying them to unreachable depths to where if I didn't uncover them, I would have eventually destroyed myself as I had almost done."

Yes, it is like the Bible says, the Word of God is like a mirror. Many do not go to the Word of God. The Word will show you who you really are and give insight to what we need from God to make our lives pleasing in His sight. But some would go to the Word or 'mirror' and straightway forget what manner of man he is. Forgetting where one came from only profits when you know God's grace has gotten you to where you are in Him. (James 1:21-25)

God does not desire for us to stay in solitude for the rest of our lives. In Genesis He said, "It is not good for man to be alone." So He gave Eve to Adam to be a helper to him. (Genesis 2:20) He said He would set the solitary in families; He'll bring out those which are bound with chains. (Psalm 68:6) Subsequently, the 'alone' time is to be used as the tool that will lose the chains and shackles that want to keep you bound to the ways of the world. Allow God to search you and reveal His innermost secrets to you. Draw near to God and He will draw near to you. Resist the devil and he will flee from you. (James 4:7-10)

OVERCOMING EVIL

For assurance in overcoming evil, the Word of God declares:

Jesus prayed that we would not be lead into temptation, but delivered from the evil one. (Matthew 6:13b, NKJV)

When the adversaries of Judah and Benjamin heard that the children of the captivity built the Temple unto the Lord God of Israel, they wanted to build with them. When Israel's leaders said no, then the people of the land weakened the hands of the people of Judah, and troubled them in building. And hired counselors against them to frustrate their purpose. (Ezra 4:1-5) Don't let the enemy frustrate your purpose!

When Sanballat heard that we were rebuilding the wall, he was furious and very indignant, and mocked the Jews. (Nehemiah 4:1, NKJV) Beware of the devices of the enemy. (2 Corinthians 2:11)

I find then a law, that when I would do good, evil is present with me. (Romans 7:21) God has given you power to overcome all the lies of the enemy. (Romans 8:37, NKJV)

Repay no one evil for evil. Have regard for good things in the sight of all men. If it is possible, as much as depends on you, live peaceably with all men. (Romans 12:17-18, NKJV)

Do not be overcome by evil, but overcome evil with good. (Romans 8:21, NKJV)

The Jews rejected the word concerning Jesus Christ, so the Apostles turned to the Gentiles. When the Gentiles heard this, "they were glad and glorified the word of the Lord.... And the word of the Lord was published throughout the whole region. But the Jews stirred up the devout and honorable women, and the chief men of the city and raised persecution against Paul and Barnabas, and expelled them out of their coasts." (Acts 13:48-50)

Jesus said, "These things I have spoken unto you that in me ye might have peace. In the world ye shall have tribulation, but be of good cheer. I have overcome the world." (John 16:33)

Paul asked the brethren to pray for him and his co-workers that they might be delivered from unreasonable and wicked men, for all men have not faith. (2 Thessalonians 3:2-3)

What persecutions I endured … and out of them all the Lord delivered me. (2 Timothy 3:11b, NKJV)

Beloved, think it not strange concerning the fiery trial which is to try you, as though some strange thing happened unto you: But rejoice, inasmuch as ye are partakers of Christ's sufferings; that, when His glory shall be revealed, ye may be glad also with exceeding joy. (1 Peter 4:12, 13, NKJV)

The Word of God is the weapon given to the believer to overcome evil and adverse circumstances. (Ephesians 6:10-18)

Hide the word in your heart, so you won't sin against Him. (Psalm 119:11)

Command your heart to believe the word and walk by faith and not by sight. (2 Corinthians 5:7)

Believe God! (Mark 11:22) You are the righteousness of God in Christ Jesus.

Section Seven

Encouraging words for personal changes

INVITATION

Dear Friend,

You are lovingly invited to enter into eternal life. The time is right now and the place is wherever you are this very moment.

You see, God so greatly loved and dearly prized the world (that's you) that He (even) gave up His only-begotten (unique) Son, so that whoever believes in (trusts, clings to, relies on) Him shall not perish (come to destruction, be lost) but have eternal, everlasting life. (John 3:16 AMP)

Look at it this way, if you have not yet received Jesus as your Savior, then you are like a man who has already been tried, judged, found guilty, sentenced, and you are now on death row – waiting to go to the electric chair.

Now, imagine someone going to that chair in your place and wiping this crime off your record. Then imagine someone coming to that prison cell, letting you know that you are now free – and all you have to do is believe that person did this for you and by believing this, walk right out of that cell door.

Well, I'm telling you that Jesus has done just that for you. He died on the cross in your place for you to be delivered from the sentence of hell, and all you have to do is believe Him and receive Him as Savior and Lord of your life.

You may say, "Well, I've never done anything to warrant this unjust sentence." I say to you, "All have sinned and come short of the glory of God." (Romans 3:23) Or you may say, "I've done too much wrong. How can God want me?" Jesus has said, "…him (or her) who comes to me, I will most certainly not cast out – I will never, no never reject one of them who comes to me." (John 6:37 AMP) For this is my Father's will and His purpose, that everyone who sees the Son and believes and cleaves to and trusts and relies on Him should have eternal life, and I will raise him up at the last day. (John 6:40 AMP)

You may even think that, I'll clean myself up, then I'll come to God. It is by free grace (God's unmerited favor) that you are saved (delivered from judgment and made partakers of Christ's salvation) through (your) faith. And this (salvation) is not of yourselves – of your own doing, it came not through your own striving – but it is the gift of God; not because of works (not the fulfillment of the Law's demands), lest any man should boast. It is not the result of what anyone can possibly do, so no one can pride himself in it or take glory to himself. (Ephesians 2:8-9 AMP)

God shows clearly, proves His (Own) love for us by the fact that while we were still sinners, Christ the Messiah, the Anointed One, died for us. (Romans 5:8)

Receive this invitation and pray with me:

Father God, thank you for loving me so much that you gave your Son to die in my place. I turn away from my sin-filled life and I receive Jesus, your free gift to me, as my Lord and Savior.
I receive the cleansing power of His blood and I am now cleansed from all sin. Jesus, thank you for coming into my life. I let you live through me. Amen.

Now go tell someone what God has done for you. Tell them it's a free gift and they are invited to receive it as well.

If you have a Bible please read: Acts 2:38-39, Acts 4:12, Romans 10:9-10, Romans 8:1, 12-17

BENEFITS WITH JESUS

Psalm 103 (MSG)

O my soul, bless GOD.
   From head to toe, I'll bless his holy name!
O my soul, bless GOD,
   don't forget a single blessing!

He forgives your sins—everyone.
He heals your diseases—everyone.
He redeems you from hell—saves your life!
He crowns you with love and mercy—a paradise crown.
He wraps you in goodness—beauty eternal.
He renews your youth—you're always young in his presence.

GOD makes everything come out right;
   he puts victims back on their feet.
He showed Moses how he went about his work,
   opened up his plans to all Israel.
GOD is sheer mercy and grace;
   not easily angered, he's rich in love.
He doesn't endlessly nag and scold,
   nor hold grudges forever.
He doesn't treat us as our sins deserve,
   nor pay us back in full for our wrongs.
As high as heaven is over the earth,
   so strong is his love to those who fear him.
And as far as sunrise is from sunset,
   he has separated us from our sins.

As parents feel for their children,
   GOD feels for those who fear him.
He knows us inside and out,
   keeps in mind that we're made of mud.
Men and women don't live very long;

like wildflowers they spring up and blossom,
But a storm snuffs them out just as quickly,
   leaving nothing to show they were here.
GOD's love, though, is ever and always,
   eternally present to all who fear him,
Making everything right for them and their children
   as they follow his Covenant ways
   and remember to do whatever he said.

GOD has set his throne in heaven;
   he rules over us all. He's the King!
So bless GOD, you angels,
   ready and able to fly at his bidding,
   quick to hear and do what he says.
Bless GOD, all you armies of angels,
   alert to respond to whatever he wills.
Bless GOD, all creatures, wherever you are—
   everything and everyone made by GOD.
And you, O my soul, bless GOD!

BE A WITNESS FOR JESUS

Calling all disciples,

In Mark 5:19 Jesus told the man to go home to thy friends and tell them…
Tell them what? That he just had an encounter with Jesus and the raging
mind and lifestyle he lived for a long time was no more. God had
compassion on him and he was no longer troubled by unclean spirits.

But ye shall receive power, after that the Holy Ghost is come upon you:
and ye shall be witnesses unto me both in Jerusalem, and in all Judea, and
in Samaria and unto the uttermost part of the earth. (Acts 1:8)

Our primary testimony should be that God has raised Jesus Christ from the
dead; and the same power that raised Christ from the dead is living in me.
The world's question is, where is God? The believer's answer is, He's in
me. That the communication of my faith becomes effectual by the
acknowledging of every good thing which is in me in Christ Jesus.
(Philemon 6) Every good thing that is in you came from God when you
believed in Jesus and confessed Him out of your mouth. For with the heart
man believes unto righteousness; and with the mouth confession is made
unto salvation. (Romans 10:10)

Jesus is not DEAD. He is definitely alive. He is alive in the Body of Christ
today. As the Body of Christ, we have been given all power and authority
to proclaim His victory over death, hell, and the grave. Other people may
give a glorious testimony and witness for Christ, but it's not until you have
a personal encounter with the Lord that you can become an effective
witness. (Matthew 28:1-10)

Do not let any of the following hindrances keep you from witnessing for
Christ:

Fear of Man:	Luke 12:8
	John 12:42-43
Love of Money:	Deuteronomy 16:19
	1 Timothy 6:10

Eating Habits:	Psalm 103:5
	Proverbs 10:11a
	Proverbs 18:20
	Proverbs 23:1-3
Sexual Desire:	2 Samuel 11:2-5
	Proverbs 6:25
	Matthew 5:27-28
	James 1:14-15

Whatever you have been delivered from, SHOUT IT from the MOUNTAIN top that JESUS IS LORD!

Humble yourselves in the sight of the Lord, and He will lift you up.
James 4:10 (NKJV)

www.ingramcontent.com/pod-product-compliance
Lightning Source LLC
Chambersburg PA
CBHW051705090426
42736CB00013B/2553